Lemonade

Victoria Blakemore

© 2018 Victoria Blakemore

All rights reserved. This book or parts thereof may not be reproduced in any form, stored in any retrieval system, or transmitted in any form by any means—electronic, mechanical, photocopy, recording, or otherwise—without prior written permission of the publisher, except as provided by United States of America copyright law. For permission requests, write to the publisher, at "Attention: Permissions Coordinator," at the address below.

vblakemore.author@gmail.com

Copyright info/picture credits

Cover, JeniFoto/Shutterstock; Page 3, jill111/Pixabay; Page 5, KikoStock/AdobeStock; Page 7, dimitrisvetsitkas1969/Pixabay; Page 9, pamela_d_mcadams/Adobestock; Page 11, Deborah Lee Roussiter/Shutterstock; Page 13, Joshua Resnick/Shutterstock; Page 15, Elena Verba/Shutterstock; Page 17, ErikaWittlieb/Pixabay; Page 19, Ryzhkov Photography/Shutterstock; Page 21, del_alma/AdobeStock; Page 23; skeeze/Pixabay; Page 25, Co-zine/AdobeStock; Page 27, mykytivoandr/AdobeStock; Page 29, Africa Studio/AdobeStock; Page 31, sveta_zarzamora/AdobeStock; Page 33, catalina.m/Shutterstock

Table of Contents

What is Lemonade?   2

Ingredients   4

Lemons   6

Where are Lemons Grown?   10

History   12

Lemonade Stands   16

Lemonade Around the World   18

Pink Lemonade   20

Nutrition   24

Health Benefits   26

Recipes   28

Glossary   34

What is Lemonade?

Lemonade is a drink that is usually made from water, lemon juice, and sugar. It can also be made from different ingredients.

Lemonade can be cloudy or clear. Clear lemonade is more like a soda. It is bubbly. In America, cloudy lemonade is more common.

The "ade" in lemonade means that it is not made completely of fruit juice.

Ingredients

In addition to lemon juice and water, lemonade is made with a sweetener. Sugar is often used. It can also be sweetened with honey.

Other fruit flavors, such as strawberry, watermelon, peach, grapefruit, or blueberry can be added to lemonade.

The lemonade often sold at lemonade stands is made from water, lemon juice, and sugar.

Lemons

Lemons grow on trees. Lemon trees are a kind of **evergreen** tree. They have leaves that stay green all year. They can also **produce** fruit all year.

Lemon trees are often grown in rows in orchards. The rows make it easy for lemons to be harvested and transported.

Lemon trees can grow many lemons. They can grow up to six hundred pounds of lemons in a single year.

Lemon trees grow from seeds. After a few years, the trees will grow flowers. If the flowers are **pollinated**, they will grow lemons. Inside the lemons are the seeds that can grow into new trees.

Lemons are a kind of citrus fruit. Other citrus fruits include oranges, grapefruits, and limes.

Like other citrus fruits, lemons have **segments** inside. When they are squeezed, the juice comes out of the **segments**.

Where are Lemons Grown?

The countries of India, Argentina, Spain, Iran, China, and the United States **produce** the most lemons in the world.

Lemons are able to be grown in many kinds of soil. They grow best in soil that is slightly **acidic**. They also need to be grown in areas that are warm.

In the United States, California and Arizona grow the most lemons. Over 58,000 acres in these two states are used for lemon orchards.

History

Lemonade is thought to have first come from Egypt over one thousand years ago.

Lemons were first grown in Asia. Ancient Egyptians mixed the lemon juice with sugar to make a drink called **qatarmizat**. The drink was sold and traded to people in other countries.

Historical records show that lemon juice was a popular item to trade in the early 1100's.

In the 1670's, lemonade became popular in Paris. It was sold on the streets. The **merchants** had containers of lemonade strapped to their backs, so they could sell it from anywhere.

In the 1830's, lemonade was first made with **carbonated** water. The bubbly drink was sold in parts of England.

In Italy, lemon juice and sugar were first frozen while they were mixed. The result was an icy cold treat called a **granita**.

Lemonade Stands

In America, lemonade stands first became popular in Brooklyn, New York in the 1870's. At the time, people could buy a glass of lemonade for as little as five cents.

Soon, lemonade stands became a popular way for children to earn money.

Lemonade stands are often seen in the summer when the weather is hot. Lemonade is very refreshing.

Lemonade Around the World

The lemonade that people drink in America is different from lemonade in other parts of the world. In parts of Europe, it is made with fizzy water, and is more like a lemon soda.

In parts of the Middle East, mint is often added to lemonade. to make a drink called limonana.

There are many **variations** of lemonade. Different fruit juices can be added to change the flavor and color.

Pink Lemonade

It is often believed that pink lemonade first came from travelling circuses. There are several stories that may explain where pink lemonade came from.

In one story, some red cinnamon candies were accidently spilled into a tub of lemonade.

It is said that the cinnamon turned the lemonade a pink color. Rather than waste it, it was sold as pink lemonade.

In the other story, the man selling lemonade at the circus ran out of water. The only water left was in a tub with the red tights worn by a performer. The water had turned pink from the red tights.

He is said to have used the pink water to make lemonade. It is not known for sure if either of these stories is completely true.

Pink lemonade often gets its color from the addition of juice made from cranberries or beets.

Nutrition

When made with freshly squeezed lemons, lemonade is full of vitamin c. It can also be a source of folate, fiber, and potassium.

Lemon juice is very low in calories and water is calorie free. Most of the calories in lemonade come from the sugar used to sweeten it.

Lemonade is healthiest when it is not made with too much sugar.

Health Benefits

When made with fresh lemons, lemonade can help you to have healthy skin and boost your immune system. This means that your body can fight germs and stay healthy.

The water in lemonade can also help you to stay **hydrated**.

The sour flavor in lemonade makes people **salivate**, which makes them feel less thirsty.

Recipes

Fresh Lemonade

Ingredients:

8 cups water   Ice

1 1/4 cups sugar

1 1/2 cups lemon juice

Directions:

1. Heat water and sugar in saucepan. Stir until sugar is dissolved.

2. Pour mixture into pitcher and add lemon juice and ice. Stir until well blended.

3. Pour into glasses and serve.

Pink Lemonade

Ingredients:

6 cups water   Ice

1 1/3 cups lemon juice

2/3 cup cranberry juice

1 1/4 cups sugar

Directions:

1. Heat water and sugar in saucepan. Stir until sugar is dissolved.

2. Pour mixture into pitcher and add lemon juice, cranberry juice, and ice. Stir until well blended.

3. Pour into glasses and serve.

Limonana

Ingredients:

4 cups water   1 cup sugar

2 cups lemon juice   Ice

1 1/2 cup mint leaves

Directions:

1. Heat 2 cups water and sugar in saucepan, stir until dissolved.

2. Combine water, lemon juice, mint leaves, and sugar mixture in blender.

3. For a slushy texture: add ice to blender.

For a juice: add ice to pitcher after the ingredients are blended.

4. Pour into glasses and serve.

Glossary

Acidic: containing acid

Carbonated: when carbon dioxide is added to water to make it bubbly

Evergreen: trees that keep their leaves all year

Granita: a dessert that is partially frozen, made from sugar, water, and fruit flavoring

Hydrated: to have enough water

Merchants: people who sell things

Pollinated: when pollen has been transferred from one plant to another, usually by bees or other insects

Produce: to make or grow

Qatarmizat: a drink Ancient Egyptians made from water, lemon juice, and sugar

Salivate: to produce extra saliva (spit)

Segments: pieces that something is separated into

Variation: different version of something

About the Author

Victoria Blakemore is a first grade teacher in Southwest Florida with a passion for reading.

You can visit her at

www.elementaryexplorers.com

Also in This Series

Also in This Series

www.ingramcontent.com/pod-product-compliance
Lightning Source LLC
Chambersburg PA
CBHW041321110526
44591CB00021B/2871